D1267145

Datos geniales sobre deportes/
Cool Sports Facts

Datos geniales sobre béisbol
Cool Baseball Facts

por/by Kathryn Clay

Editora consultora/Consulting Editor:
Gail Saunders-Smith, PhD

Consultor/Consultant: Craig Coenen, PhD
Profesor Adjunto de Historia/Associate Professor of History
Mercer County Community College
West Windsor, New Jersey

CAPSTONE PRESS
a capstone imprint

Pebble Plus is published by Capstone Press,
1710 Roe Crest Drive, North Mankato, Minnesota 56003.
www.capstonepub.com

Library of Congress Cataloging-in-Publication Data
Clay, Kathryn.
[Cool baseball facts. Spanish.]
Datos geniales sobre béisbol = Cool baseball facts / by Kathryn Clay.
p. cm. —(Pebble plus bilingue/bilingual)
Includes index.
ISBN 978-1-4296-9217-5 (library binding)
ISBN 978-1-62065-337-1 (ebook PDF)
1. Baseball—Miscellanea—Juvenile literature. I. Title.
GV867.5.C53 2013
796.357—dc23 2011050104

Summary: Simple text and full-color photos illustrate facts about the rules, equipment, and records of baseball.

Editorial Credits
Erika L. Shores, editor; Strictly Spanish, translation services; Kyle Grenz, designer; Eric Manske, bilingual book designer and production specialist; Eric Gohl, media researcher

Photo Credits
AP Images/Chris O'Meara, 7; Richard Lui, 5
Corbis/Reuters/Sam Mircovich, 17
Dreamstime/Lawrence Weslowski Jr., cover
Getty Images Inc./Pool, 21; Sports Imagery/Ronald C. Modra, 19
The Granger Collection, New York, 9
MLB Photos via Getty Images/Arizona Diamondbacks/Jonathan Willey, 11; Rich Pilling, 15
Shutterstock/Adrian Coroama, cover (baseball), back cover, 1; Ken Inness, 13

The author dedicates this book to her dad, a lifelong Minnesota Twins fan.

Note to Parents and Teachers

The Datos geniales sobre deportes/Cool Sports Facts series supports national social studies standards related to people, places, and culture. This book describes and illustrates baseball. The images support early readers in understanding the text. The repetition of words and phrases helps early readers learn new words. This book also introduces early readers to subject-specific vocabulary words, which are defined in the Glossary section. Early readers may need assistance to read some words and to use the Table of Contents, Glossary, Internet Sites, and Index sections of the book.

Printed in the United States of America in North Mankato, Minnesota.
042012 006682CGF12

Table of Contents

Tabla de contenidos

Home Run!

More than 70 million fans go to MLB games each year. These fans eat 30 million hot dogs while watching their favorite teams.

¡Cuadrangular!

Más de 70 millones de aficionados van a los juegos de las MLB cada año. Estos aficionados comen 30 millones de perros calientes mientras ven a sus equipos favoritos.

MLB stands for Major League Baseball.

MLB son las siglas en inglés de las Grandes Ligas de Béisbol.

Cool Equipment

Baseballs are rubbed
with mud before games.
It makes the balls
easier to throw.

Equipo genial

Antes de cada partido,
las pelotas de béisbol son
frotadas con lodo.
Así es más fácil lanzar las pelotas.

OFFICIAL BALL
2008 WORLD SERIES

The first official uniform
was worn in 1849.
The Knickerbockers wore
blue pants, white shirts,
and straw hats.

El primer uniforme oficial se
usó en 1849.
Los Knickerbockers vestían
pantalones azules, camisetas
blancas y sombreros de paja.

Cool Rules

Batters don't always need to hit the ball to reach base. Getting hit by a pitch sends the batter to first base.

Reglas geniales

Los bateadores no siempre tienen que golpear la pelota para llegar a la base. Si un bateador es golpeado por un lanzamiento, va a primera base.

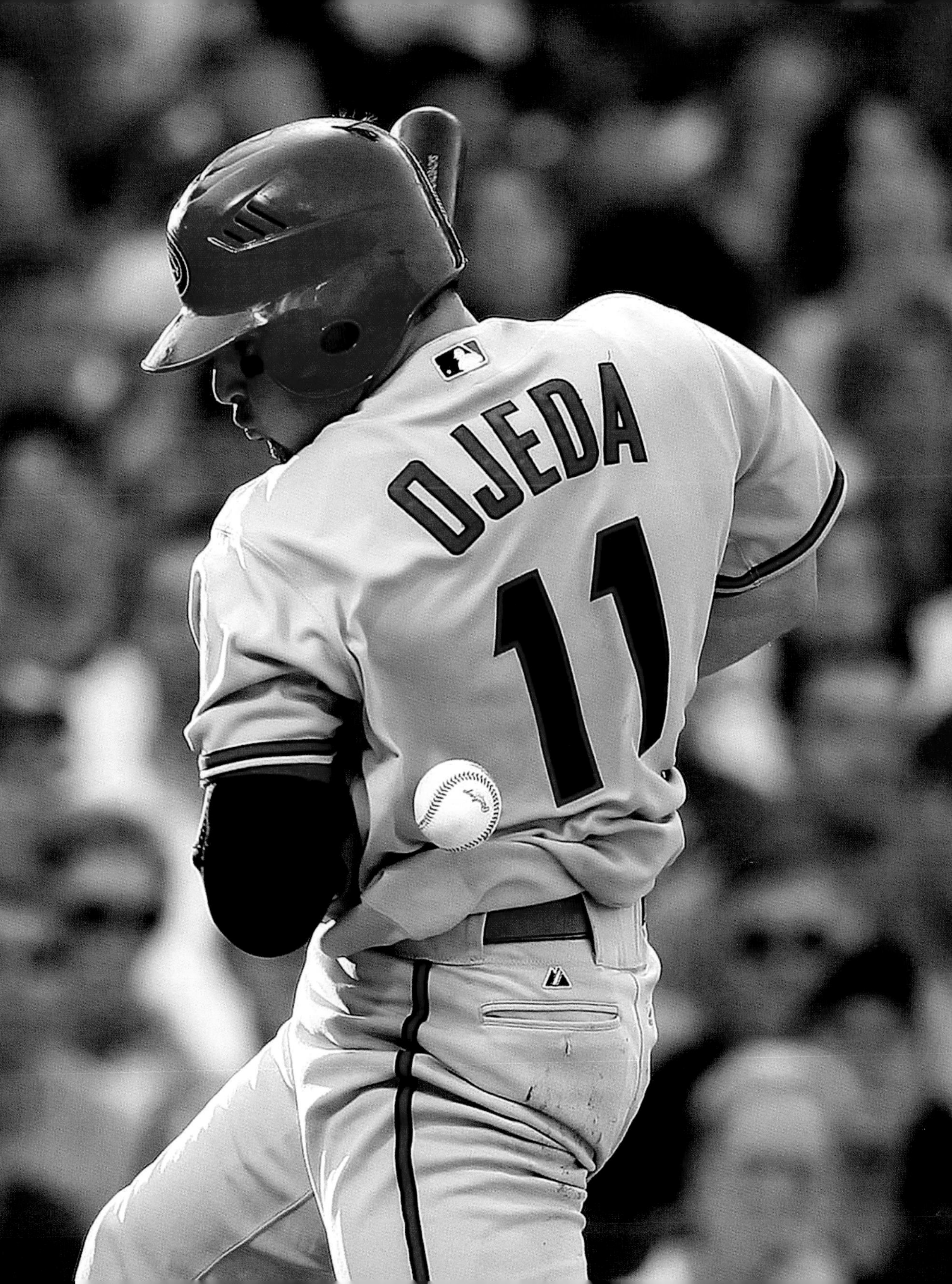
OJEDA
11

It's against the rules
for a pitcher to spit on the ball.
A pitcher also can't rub
a ball on his glove or clothing.

Es contra las reglas que el lanzador
escupa sobre la pelota.
Tampoco se permite que un lanzador
frote la pelota en su guante o en su ropa.

HK

Cool Records

In his career, Nolan Ryan pitched seven games without giving up a hit. No other pitcher has thrown as many no-hitters.

Récords geniales

En su carrera, Nolan Ryan lanzó siete juegos sin dar un solo hit. Ningún otro lanzador ha lanzado tantos juegos sin hit.

T
34

Only one player has ever hit two grand slams in the same inning. Fernando Tatis did it on April 23, 1999.

Solo un jugador ha hecho dos grand slams en la misma entrada. Fernando Tatis lo hizo el 23 de abril de 1999.

#1
#2

Baltimore Orioles shortstop Cal Ripken Jr., didn't miss a game in 16 years.
He played 2,632 games in a row.

El parador en corto de los Orioles de Baltimore, Cal Ripken Jr., no faltó a ningún partido en 16 años.
Jugó 2,632 juegos seguidos.

The New York Yankees
have won 27 World Series.
The St. Louis Cardinals have
the second most titles with 11.

Los Yanquis de Nueva York han
ganado 27 Series Mundiales.
Los Cardenales de San Luis tienen la
segunda mayoría de títulos, con 11.

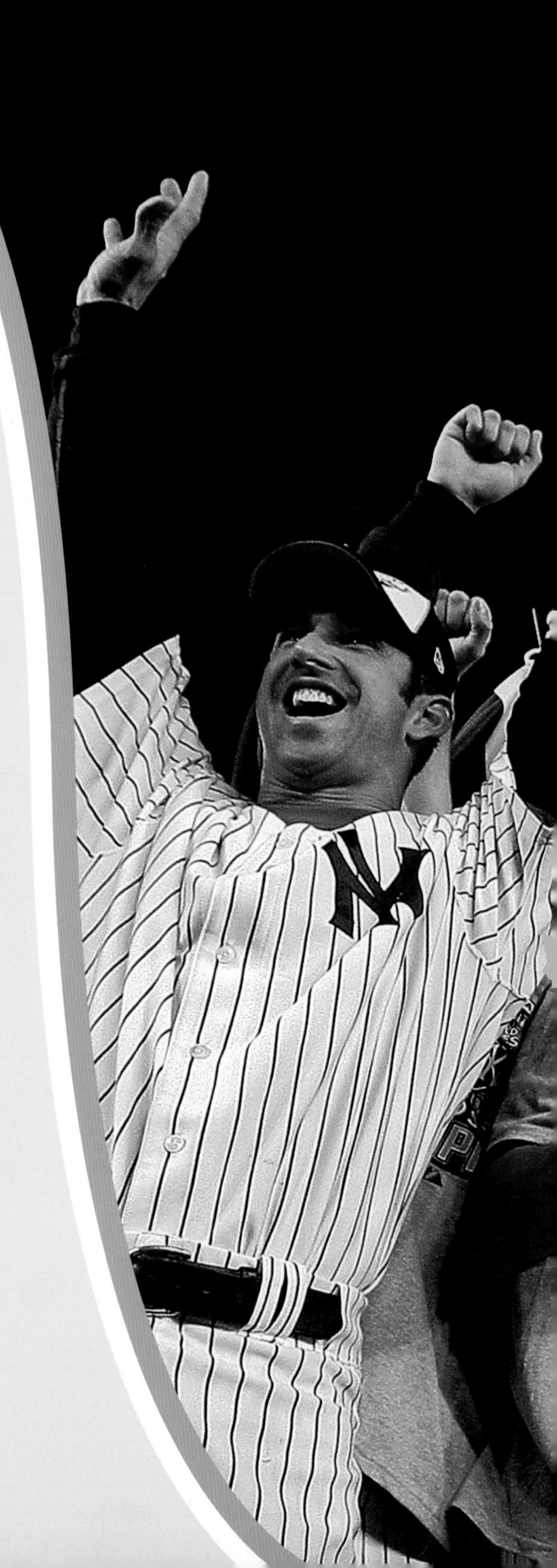

Glossary

batter—the person whose turn it is to bat

grand slam—to hit a home run when there is a runner on every base

inning—part of a baseball game when each team gets a turn to bat; a baseball game has nine innings

no-hitter—a game in which no batter gets on base by hitting the ball; a batter can reach base in a no-hitter by walking or if the other team makes an error

pitch—a baseball thrown to the batter

shortstop—the position between second and third base

Internet Sites

FactHound offers a safe, fun way to find Internet sites related to this book. All of the sites on FactHound have been researched by our staff.

Here's all you do:

Visit *www.facthound.com*

Type in this code: 9781429692175

Glosario

el bateador—la persona que tiene su turno al bate

la entrada—parte de un partido de béisbol en la que cada equipo tiene turno al bate; un partido de béisbol tiene nueve entradas

el grand slam—hacer un jonrón cuando hay un corredor en cada base

el juego sin hit—juego en el que ningún bateador llega a la base por golpear la pelota; el bateador puede llegar a la base en un juego sin hit por bases por bola o si el otro equipo comete un error

el lanzamiento—una pelota de béisbol lanzada al bateador

el parador en corto—la posición entre segunda y tercera base

Sitios de Internet

FactHound brinda una forma segura y divertida de encontrar sitios de Internet relacionados con este libro. Todos los sitios en FactHound han sido investigados por nuestro personal.

Esto es todo lo que tienes que hacer:

Visita *www.facthound.com*

Ingresa este código: 9781429692175

Index

Índice